TI-Bmy - 879

Washington

The Evergreen State

Tika Downey

PowerKiDS press™

New York

Published in 2010 by The Rosen Publishing Group, Inc.
29 East 21st Street, New York, NY 10010

First Edition

Editor: Joanne Randolph
Book Design: Greg Tucker
Photo Researcher: Jessica Gerweck

Photo Credits: Cover, pp. 9, 13, 15, 22 (amphibian) Shutterstock.com; p. 5 © Kevin Schafer/Corbis; p. 7 MPI/Getty Images; p. 11 © www.istockphoto.com/Martin Dollenkamp; p. 17 © Michael T. Sedam/ Corbis; p. 19 © www.istockphoto.com/Jeremy Edwards; p. 22 (tree) Tom Bean/Getty Images; p. 22 (bird) © www.istockphoto.com/Frank Leung; p. 22 (flower) © www.istockphoto.com/Mike Bentley; p. 22 (Chief Seattle) © Museum of History and Industry/Corbis; p. 22 (Linda Buck) Win McNamee/Getty Images; p. 22 (Bill Gates) Chris Hondros/Getty Images.

Library of Congress Cataloging-in-Publication Data

Downey, Tika.
 Washington : the Evergreen State / Tika Downey. — 1st ed.
    p. cm. — (Our amazing states)
 Includes index.
 ISBN 978-1-4042-8113-4 (library binding) — ISBN 978-1-4358-3346-3 (pbk.) — ISBN 978-1-4358-3347-0 (6-pack)
 1. Washington (State)—Juvenile literature. I. Title.
 F891.3.D69 2010
 979.7—dc22

                                        2009002892

Manufactured in the United States of America

Contents

The Evergreen State

You know that the United States' first president was George Washington, right? He became president in 1789, six years after our country won its freedom from British rule. Our nation's capital, Washington, D.C., was named in his honor. Washington State was, too. In fact, Washington is the only state named after a president.

Washington is in the northwestern corner of the United States and is famous for its many kinds of natural beauty. It has a coast on the Pacific Ocean, high mountains, green valleys, and land so dry that it is almost a desert. Its large forests filled with **evergreen** trees gave the state its nickname, the Evergreen State.

Puget Sound, shown here, lies in northwestern Washington, between the Olympic and Cascade mountains. The sound is an estuary, where salt water and freshwater come together.

Early Days

Washington's first people were Native Americans who likely crossed the **Bering Land Bridge** from Asia to America thousands of years ago. Today many different tribes made their homes in Washington.

English **explorer** Captain James Cook reached the area in 1778. After visits by English explorer George Vancouver and American fur trader Robert Gray in 1792, fur trading with Native Americans became important.

Missionaries started coming in the early 1800s. By the 1840s, American settlers were arriving after a hard journey across the country by wagon train. After a cross-country railroad was finished in 1883, the number of settlers grew quickly. Just six years later, Washington became the forty-second state.

Until around 1849, Fort Vancouver was the center of a huge fur-trading business run by a British company. More than 61,000 animal skins were sent to Britain in 1843 alone.

America's Rain Forest

Washington's rainy weather is famous. Did you know that the state has rain forests, though? It is true! They are in the Olympic Mountains, on the Olympic **Peninsula**, which is between the Pacific Ocean and Puget Sound. Puget Sound is a long bay with many harbors. Winds bring rain to western Washington from the Pacific Ocean. However, that rain does not reach eastern Washington because the Cascade Mountains block it.

The Cascade Mountains got their name from the many cascades, or short, steep waterfalls, in the Columbia River **Gorge**. The river runs along most of Washington's southern border and separates it from Oregon.

These moss-covered trees grow in Washington's Hoh Rain Forest, which is part of Olympic National Park. Washington's rain forests can get up to 12 feet (4 m) of rain each year!

Wild and Wonderful

Washington's rain forests have lots of evergreen trees as well as maple trees, mosses, and wildflowers. The drier, eastern part of Washington has desert plants, such as grasses and sagebrush.

All sorts of animals live in Washington's different **habitats**. There are bears, deer, bobcats, and mountain goats. There are also smaller animals such as beavers, minks, birds, and fish.

One animal found throughout Washington is the state **amphibian**, the tiny Pacific chorus frog. Can you guess why it is called a chorus frog? This frog sings! It uses a special pouch in its throat to make beautiful songs.

The Pacific chorus frog was picked as Washington's state amphibian in 2007. The small frog, which has a black stripe on each side of its head, is known for its beautiful calls.

Mighty Mount Rainier

The Cascade Mountains run through Washington from north to south. Many of the mountains are **volcanoes**, including Mount St. Helens, which **erupted** in 1980.

One of the most famous volcanoes is Mount Rainier. It is the highest mountain in Washington. Mount Rainier is 14,410 feet (4,392 m) tall. That is almost 2.75 miles (4.5 km)! The last time Mount Rainier erupted was 150 years ago.

Because Mount Rainier is so tall, its top is very cold. There are 26 major glaciers, or huge sheets of ice, covering its upper parts year round. Trees, flowers, and many kinds of animals live on the mountain's lower parts.

Here you can see Mount Rainier's snowy peak. The largest glacier on Mount Rainier is Emmons Glacier, which has 4.3 square miles (11 sq km) of ice.

Working in Washington

With all those forests, it is not surprising that many Washington businesses make and sell lumber, paper, and other wood products, or goods. The state's many rivers and lakes and the Pacific Ocean make fishing an important business. All that water serves another purpose, too. With it, Washington produces about one-third of all the **hydroelectricity** in the United States!

Farming is also important in Washington. Apples, potatoes, and wheat are some of the main crops grown there.

Washington is famous for its factories. These factories make many different products, such as airplanes, ships, and computers. Many other Washington companies make computer **software**.

Washington grows more apples than any other state, picking enough to fill around 100 million boxes each year. Out of every 10 apples you eat, 6 are likely from Washington.

Come See Olympia

Olympia, which is on Puget Sound, is Washington's capital and an important harbor. Huge ships come there to carry away logs, lumber, and other goods made in Washington.

Settlers began arriving in Washington in the 1840s. The U.S. government made Washington an official U.S. territory in 1853 and made Isaac Stevens the territory's governor. Stevens named Olympia the capital. The city remained the capital when Washington became a state in 1889.

You can learn about Olympia's history at **museums** downtown. There is Bigelow House, which was the home of one of the city's early leaders, and the Washington State Capital Museum.

Washington's state capitol, built in 1928, has the fourth-tallest stone dome in the world. It also has the largest number of solar panels of any U.S. capitol, with 144 panels on its roof.

The Space Needle

Do you know what the Space Needle in Seattle is? It sounds as if it has something to do with space travel. The Space Needle will not be blasting off, though. It is a building.

The Space Needle was built for the 1962 world's fair. The people who planned the building wanted it to stand for the great things Americans hoped to accomplish one day, such as space travel. That is why it looks the way it does. It is reaching for the stars! The Space Needle is 605 feet (184 m) tall.

The Space Needle is one of Washington's most famous buildings. More than one million people visit it every year. Many go to the top to enjoy the view of the city.

The Space Needle was the tallest building west of the Mississippi River when it was built in 1962. There are 848 steps from the Space Needle's basement to its observation deck.

Welcome to Washington

Many visitors go to Washington to enjoy its beautiful green places. You can go camping or fishing, walk in rain forests, or climb to the top of mountains. In winter, you can enjoy sports such as skiing or snowboarding.

You can visit a city such as Seattle or Tacoma while in Washington. You can learn about Washington's past at Fort Vancouver, which was founded in 1825 as a supply post for a fur-trading company. The state also has several museums that teach about Washington's history. There are art and science museums, too. There is even a museum about airplane history! What would you like to do in Washington?

amphibian (am-FIH-bee-un) An animal that spends the first part of its life in water and the rest on land.

Bering Land Bridge (BAYR-ing LAND BRIJ) The strip of land that at one time formed a bridge or means of crossing from Siberia to Alaska, where the Bering Strait is today.

erupted (ih-RUP-ted) Sent gases, smoke, or lava from inside a volcano up into the air.

evergreen (EH-ver-green) A shrub or tree that has green leaves or needles all year.

explorer (ek-SPLOR-ur) A person who travels and looks for new land.

gorge (GORJ) A steep, narrow passage through land.

habitats (HA-buh-tats) The places in which plants and animals naturally live.

hydroelectricity (hy-droh-ih-lek-TRIH-suh-tee) Electricity made from water.

missionaries (MIH-shuh-ner-eez) People sent to another country to tell people about a certain faith.

museums (myoo-ZEE-umz) Places where art or historical pieces are safely kept for people to see and to study.

peninsula (peh-NIN-suh-luh) An area of land surrounded by water on three sides.

software (SOFT-wayr) Computer applications, or special files, that are made to do certain tasks.

volcanoes (vol-KAY-nohz) Openings in the surface of Earth that sometimes shoot up a hot liquid rock called lava.

Washington State Symbols

State Tree
Western
Hemlock

State Amphibian
Pacific Chorus
Frog

State Flag

State Bird
Willow Goldfinch

State Flower
Coast
Rhododendron

State Seal

Famous People from Washington

Chief Seattle
(c. 1786–1866)
Born near
Blake Island, WA
Leader of the Squamish
and Duwamish tribes

Linda Buck
(1947–)
Born in Seattle, WA
Nobel-Prize-Winning
Biologist

Bill Gates
(1955–)
Born in Seattle, WA
Businessman/Chairman
of Microsoft

Washington State Map

Bellingham

Olympic Mountains

Puget Sound

Lake Washington

Seattle

Olympia ⊛

Tacoma

Cascade Mountains

Columbia River

Lake Franklin D. Roosevelt

Yakima River

Wenatchee

Spokane

Yakima

Columbia River Basin

Snake River

Kennewick

Columbia River

Legend

○ Major City

⊛ Capital

〜 River

Washington State Facts

Population: About 6,549,224

Area: About 68,192 square miles (176,616 sq km)

Motto: "Alki," a Chinook Indian word that means "by and by"

Song: "Washington, My Home," written by Helen Davis and arranged by Stuart Churchill

Index

Web Sites

Due to the changing nature of Internet links, PowerKids Press has developed an onli
list of Web sites related to the subject of this book. This site is updated regularly.
Please use this link to access the list:
www.powerkidslinks.com/amst/wa/

404